Earthly
Conventions

EARTHLY CONVENTIONS

First published by Egg Box Publishing 2023
Part of UEA Publishing Project Ltd
International ©2023 retained by individual authors

Earthly Conventions is typeset in Baskerville Regular 10.5pt

Design and Typeset Rebekah Sinclair
Cover Illustration by Gemma Pugh
Proofread by Elizabeth Yew

Printed and bound in the UK by Lightning Source
Distributed by Egg Box Publishing

ISBN 978-1-915812-29-2

The University of East Anglia's Creative Writing
Society Anthology 2022/23

Earthly Conventions

A collection of prose and poetry by students from
The University of East Anglia

* * *

Dear reader,

In your hands you find a delectable collection of
literary morsels, a spread of UEA's finest cuisine.
We have temperate hot air balloons and piranhas
and unwashed socks, misty September mornings and
national rail symphonies; whatever your palate, from
plush boudoirs to fallen stars, there is something in this
collection to whet your appetite. So now is the time to
abandon your earthly conventions and to indulge.

Happy feasting,

UEA's very own CWS

Contents

CHARLIE MOORLAND

The City Blocks

Content Warning: Death

Soundproof sheltering dials rattle from minor impacts. Another accolade
of the dismayed scamper off, out of the closet, collapsing their tower and
breathing pocket. Its aftershocks reverberate, a gentle lullaby echoes.
A sound fills the street, a screech of shattering glass and tarmac. Four city
blocks away, another 'skyscraper' has gone up in flames. Sighing can be
heard from apartments above and so is echoed below.

Their words hold no pertinence, to my lucid denial. Those people haven't
died, they've just escaped. To a deeper, warmer, lighter place. The flames
lick all around, swiftly doused by streams of concrete flowers, that bloom
up like mangroves and twist into new-found home bowers. Minutes scarcely
pass, in the wake of time mislaid, and the tower is replenished.

The warm dreams vanquished, the martyr's soul sacrifice annihilated.
I would cry out in anguish, if my voice hadn't atrophied in the
punitive silence.

You have to remember the positives. More people live now than ever before,
swelled by increased fertility rates. Humans have always, ironically, bred like
rabbits. Oh, I do remember the days, when young people were so frightened
of intimacy, so shunned from care, their parents and leaders and racing
hares telling them — *STOP. KEEP AT WORK. DON'T STRAY FROM THE
WAY.* Now nobody has to work, and the foundry machine, filled with the
nectar of human regeneration, plops out newborn babes, every second, of
every day. Children fill every apartment block, hoarded in neat, regimented
supplies. Handed out to the desperate, the needy, the hungry and the greedy.
And if an apartment block crumbles, or a catwalk system of towns tumbles,

or a tower jumbles itself into a ball of rage and alights — then all need not fear. The surface, for but a brief moment uncovered, hiding the rot of hidden, unbidden life, will be swiftly covered. By a new layer of concrete.

What pitiful dross!

Such a system confounds all natural laws. How can a child sit in joy, if its sights are naught but a steel board, ever present glass alighted with the ethereal strings of images unbound and unsound? Satire has become reality, he was right, that aged scholar of centuries now discarded and gainfully hollered away to rich termite scrivens and archivists and noble piles of detritus, children have become naught but food-stuffs. Plentiful as the cities that, like cancerous growths, rupture from the ground of waste and scrap rust. Of dust and bitter musk.

I have recently had a check-up, myself being wheeled into the Eastern wing of this city block's hospital 'thing'. The walls are translucent, anti-bacterial plastic shells that harden to the approach of hateful microbes and excrete sanitary solutions to all that within dwell. Steep stairs, fit for the healthy, stack up like ant tunnels, perforating the complex of rising rooms. Through the walls, one can see the outside landscape, that forever hell. A black dressed nurse had to scan my flesh, as I neared the entrance way. I wonder if the walls consider me a pathogen, something to be barred and kept away. The doctor greets me, with his stick thin, insectile gait, needles his way inside my flesh, and sends me on my way. I do not have cancer, any impairment of the body or liquidation of the brain. Yet all the same, I shudder in this nightmare, and wonder: Is it I or the world that has gone insane?

Wandering the city blocks, I approach a highway, one in a million that crisscross my home state. The vehicles all look the same, passing under the ghost light of the false night, a dark malaise of oblong objects that race hitherto and from every conceivable place and space. The pavement feels so small, like a thin wire that I balanced on from my youngest dream. If I fall, I'll be severed into a trillion-fold pieces. My body erased.

False night awakens to the shade of my apartment hiding place. It is near the ground floor of building 14167814. Vast and spacious, I have a considerable amount of living space. The walls press flavoured colours into the recesses of my brain: the cool tranquillity of blue, the gushing warmth of red, the vaunted heights of purple and the green grass of home. All swirl into a cavalcade of memories, overbearing and agonising, yet so treasured and dear. Solely, the notepad afront me reads as follows:

<u>The Vanished Shade</u>

The forest has alighted,

The seas absconded from their depths,

The sky has lost its perch,

The birds and fish and forest creatures have been decimated,

Pushed into the blighted folds of forgotten histories,

I remember the green of home,

The purple vanity of those above and so below,

The red warmth of a smile,

That even now as memories picture…turns to ruin and sourness bitter,

The coolness of the pool,

Now buried under mounds of infinite concrete,

Its surface moulded and gangrenous,

A fetid well of once joyful belongings,

Now I sit in a vaunted cell,

A city block raised above and past and out of sight of the stars themselves,

'Neath nothing and no-one,

Not God, or Earth or the Madmen of yesteryear,

Only the vanished shade,

Looks down onto our Immensity,

And utters a wordless prayer, or request or mindless statement to the non-air,

'The lights will go out, and the concrete and all within will disappear,

Into dust and depths, of brighter hopes and brighter cheers.'

Into the silent bliss of yesterdays' years.

DANIEL GARCIA

Away

Content Warning: Mild violence

Faster than all light and sound,
Through morning mist and sunlit sands,
And blood-soaked roses digging into your flesh
Mercilessly. You are long past the point of no return
And it hurts. But still you do it —
Veins pumping ichor and scalding venom
On an orphic journey into your very own Tartarus.
Your memory breathes with every jolt;
Every wayward leap sets your heart ablaze,
Flings you further into reverent oblivion.

It is so romantically human
To be loved.
It is so romantically human
To run.

Ariel Gets Fired

The five had started to feel like a family recently. Not so much like a mother and a father and two kids and a dog, but in the way that they were always around each other, spent every waking second breathing each other's air so much that at some point their DNA had begun to mix into some strange co-operative home. Sometimes, the in-laws would visit — Dion would often open the door to the parents of one of the others and have to entertain them with cheap instant coffee and regale them with stories of WeHo, jumping into damage control mode when he'd pushed it too far. *Oh, I was joking! No, no, I was exaggerating! Did I say boyfriend? I meant to say girlfriend, yes, girlfriend.* He'd even learned Spanish to try and squeeze an inch of respect out of Ricky's mother.

And like all families, they made a tradition out of terse meals at just-left-of-good restaurants, their favourite being some Cantonese place in Sunset Plaza. It was 'some place' because they knew how to get to it, and it had a particular smell of deep-fry and barbecue sauce that made the name secondary. It was typical — brightly lit with all-white everything, like a bathroom; disposable tissue tablecloths; little glass dishes with tealights; ceramic tea sets with piping hot green tea and warm lemon water on each table. While the tablecloths were disposable, the menus were all laminated and stacked tight in a holder at the centre of the table. They had their rituals: Ricky beside Dion, beside Sandy opposite Ariel beside Michael. Ariel picked up a menu and fanned away the sweat on his brow.

"I got fired."
Sandy put her glass down and swallowed hard. "For what?"

"I don't know," Ariel said.
"You brought it up."

He scratched the back of his neck and hid his face with the menu,
"Do they only do char siu with pork?" Sandy leaned back in her chair. She
shot a glance at the other three, a 'back me up' sort of look. Ricky was at
the head of the table, waving his hand over the tealight candle, getting closer
each time, until the flame licked the skin of his palm and he drew it away.
Dion was mouthing along emphatically to Wet Willie's 'Keep On Smilin'.
The restaurant owner had a strange affinity for blues. Michael was actually
reading the menu. She let him off the hook, assuming that he truly had no
clue what was going on.

"How are we gonna make rent?"
"You could apply for unemployment while you wait." Sandy suggested.
They all laughed.
"Char siu chicken, two or three fried rice?"
"Three!" Ricky slapped his pack of cigarettes down on the table.
He drew one out and lit it on the tealight. He let it burn for a second, as
if he had something else to add, but then he put it to his mouth and
murmured, "Three."

Dion swung back and forth on his chair, "You know, you are so nihilistic.
Flow on with the changes! Until the sun comes out again!" He slammed his palm
on the table as the chair came cascading down on the ground with a thud.
"Maybe he'll get a better paying job. Fuck Amnesty International. I mean,
what are they gonna do without you?"

Ariel smiled, "I think Amnesty International will survive without me hocking
Bob Dylan biographies."

"We need to push harder with the clubs. I'm serious. They're the only choice."
Ricky looked between Dion, who was most likely to back him up because
he always did; and Ariel, who loved to push the defeatist idea that he was
wasting his life.

Sandy sighed. "We just need to focus on the cash right now. We're just
getting by. But we're working, we're saving at least a little — "

"If we work the clubs hard enough, we'll never need to focus on the cash ever again!" Ricky was wide eyed, waving his smoke around, flicking hot ash across the table. It melted into the tablecloth.

"That's a big 'if'."
"And we can order four tubs of fried rice, or even go somewhere nicer!" A glowing shard of ash flew across the room and clung to the back of a little girl's sweater. "Shut up, man." Michael shot a horrified look over to the owner at the till, who very much did not care about an overblown, self-aggrandizing wannabe rockstar's opinion of his restaurant.

The girl's mother gasped and patted the ash down. She glared at Ricky, who gave her a wink. "He's right." Ariel argued, "I didn't pass up Brandeis-Bardin to bum around working at every sex shop on the Strip. A man can only take so much 'Darling Nikki'."

"Ain't that the truth." Dion concurred.

Sandy clenched her fist, "Fucking — if I ever hear the words Brandeis-Bardin again I'm gonna..." she grumbled to herself. "Whatever. Whatever. We can talk to some clubs, that won't hurt, but we can't afford to rent out any rehearsal space. We'll have to do it at home, which means we'll have to keep it down."

"No!" Ariel, Ricky, and Dion exclaimed in unison.

"We will!" Sandy insisted, pointing an accusatory finger at Ricky. There was a mother in this family, and a gaggle of children. Just no father and no dog (unless you count cockroaches). She felt a pang of frustration. Mother was no fun. But little sister was. She lowered her finger slowly, transforming her scowl into a sad furrowed brow. "I just...I don't want to get kicked out again. Is that too much to ask?"

"No!" all four cried out this time, imbued with a righteous need to protect her, or this fraudulent side of her.

It's that easy, she thought, God, I do love them.

FIONA HILL

Meeting September

September met me lonely at the crossroads,
Stranded in the dim for the first time in nineteen years,
She was fading too and it showed,
By the musty smoke-smell on her breath,

I heard she has passed on now,
You know she left without speaking a word?
Though I scavenge for the rasp of her voice,
She lies paralysed in photographs, dying in the blur,

I track through the aisles we strode down,
To the same shrill of the radiator's laugh,
And find ghosts of her buried in bookshelves,
Laid to rest by the roosting from the park,

The wind finds reason to echo
Our long nights in the din of September,
Bristling my skin through this concrete throw
I curled up in, when I couldn't remember,

The sweetness of unbaked shortbread,
Endless summer, so sure of its purpose,
Scents of cordial entwined in the garden shed,
And it was endearing to be somewhat nervous,

But September — today I'll still listen,
Filter out whispers of pages and coughs,
And sketch your skyline on the back of my journal,
Shading in the soon-to-be-forgot.

FIONA HILL

Tuesday 13th December 2022: The Day Before it Snowed

This morning, I take myself, sleepy-eyed, on a walk 'round Earlham Hall,
The crisp, thin December air shakes the duvet off my bones
as I make my way,
In frost, the wraith of dew, and become a visitant of the Dutch Garden,
The pines, the common land.
The heavens. Shift in shades of vivid blue as I tuck my fingers in my sleeves.

Stopping by the garden wall, I let myself remember my childhood,
In streaks of sunlight that stand, thoughtful, in the places
I had made other stories,
Birthed other people; the flickering shards of me.
Today. I come across a way to view the present as dim,
Or at least false, as I see my past in glassy ghosts, clear in stone about me,
So lucid, I lose myself and glare at anyone who touches them,

I listen for the cackle of the furl of leaves below my feet,
On pathways created by their tread, guarded by crows they welcome me
Home. The past few months I've spent watching crows,
Diving out of the grey of seven floors tall. Pretence,
The longer I gazed, the stronger I thought my look would fit,
A romance. Now I watch them just for me.

I am not one to let moments slip through my fingers,
But I know now that nine o'clock will shift suddenly to ten,
And as I take myself on a walk 'round Earlham Hall this morning,
I feel my lungs tighten as the bitter chill races through my chest,
And I want to return to today. That hot place,
Drunk on the now, steeped in movement,
Not yet beautiful, not yet my own, unfiltered in the pallid glaze.
Raw. For that, I'd let everything I have, here, this very past, thaw.

INGRID MARIE JENSEN

Good News

Content Warning: Self-harm

The morning light slices into my retinas. It's too early for this. The older
I get, the better hibernation sounds. But instead of being at home in bed
hiding snugly from the future and the past and the place in between,
I'm standing on the Millennium Bridge with Evangeline. It was her idea.
Hanging out on a freezing, wind-whipped outlook over a pollution-choked
river at 10 a.m. on a Saturday morning; this is the sort of thing she likes
to do, the sort of thing that gets her through a week of her retail job in the
capitalist hell of the Westfield shopping centre.

Today, on her day off, she's wearing stupid kitschy sunglasses with
heart-shaped lenses, microscopic shorts and a voluminous black hoodie that
covers the shorts, making it look like she doesn't even have any on.
She'd gotten the once-over in the queue at Gregg's earlier. Some guy old
enough to be her dad. He had slipped his tongue from between his parched
and flaking grey lips, wet pink tongue like the tip of a dog's dick. I'd glared
at him, stabbed two fingers upwards and mouthed a few choice words:
fuck off, get lost, die. When 'the fire next time' everyone's always talking
about finally comes, it'll consume him. Worms eating and shitting his sorry
bones to dust.

Evangeline's oblivious to the million offences I continually see being levelled
against her by the glances of passing strangers. Gulping her coffee, leaning
against the bridge railing with her full weight, placing a level of trust in civil
engineers that I wouldn't place in God. I grab her hood, pull her back.
Her crooked front teeth, lips parted in a belly-laugh, short white-blonde
hair blowing in the wind like electrical sparks. Evangeline, my best friend,
who got me through lockdown alive, who's served more of a purpose in my

life than most girls I have a reason to remember, and who's now just a little
too hard to handle. Too much trouble since she conjured that white-blonde
hair up out of a bottle. *Goodbye, Evangeline*: the title of the movie that's been
playing in my head for weeks. Haven't been able to get the credits to roll yet;
can't seem to stop the film from rolling, it just keeps on.

Evangeline settles down to watch the river churning past below, crooked
sharp teeth tearing at a vegan sausage roll. I stop gulping coffee long enough
to split the silence with a warning — don't be dropping your breakfast into
the river, miss. There's enough crap in it as it stands, doesn't need your litter,
too. *Vee-gan*, she says, parroting that video of Boris Johnson, aiming a kick at
my shins, *vee-gan*. She grins, loves an in-joke, does Evangeline.

Me+Evangeline=HAPPY. We've been a nice, well-balanced equation, but
equations are for school kids, aren't they? And I'm a man grown, 24, with
a degree and a job and a room in Bethnal Green to my name. No mean feat
these days, in this social-political climate. Evangeline's a woman grown,
too, but who wants to tell her? She's 20 and she still has ideas about who
and what she wants to be next week, continually playing dress-up with her
own myriad personalities. I wish she was either always joking or never joking,
because it's so hard to tell the difference.

Here's a piece of good news, Evangeline says. It's no longer biologically
dead. The Thames, I mean. Who knew a river could die, I say and she says
"mm, this other river in Ohio, in America, it caught on fire once..."
Oh, well, I interrupt. An American river, what do you expect, of course it
doesn't know how fucking behave itself decently. She bursts into giggles,
says you always make me laugh, despite the pain.

I fart.

It's fear. Fear of this present state of happiness melting away, washing away
like the flakes of *vee-gan sossie roll* Evangeline is crumbling slyly into the
grey river. Fear that walking the line, keeping the distance, will get too hard.
It's already too hard. The white-blonde hair, the insolence, the interest in
anything that's depressing as fuck — Blixa Bargeld, pale, platinum-haired
folk singers in skeleton suits, the end of the world, and this zombie of a river.
Cynicism is only for the very young, the hatchlings. Fear and lust are what's

left for the space in limbo. Fear and lust consume me, shove me roughly beneath the ground Evangeline dances lightly over. Consumed by fear, the worst thing. Can't risk it anymore; I'm done.

Evangeline pulls her hood up, jerks the strings tight around her cheeks, which are still soft with puppy fat like a Christmas cherub. All the fat gone from everywhere else. A limby miracle. A constant worry. I'd have slit my wrists long ago, working at Westfield. I hand her my *vee-gan sossie roll*, with instructions: *EAT*. She looks up over her stupid heart-shaped sunglasses, squints, smiles at the big-brother routine. She takes a bite, says *CHOMP* with cartoonish volume, makes me take a bite, says *CHOMP* on my behalf, laughs, snaps a photo. She sticks it up on Insta and adds a **#besties** caption for irony, but we both know it's true. Evangeline does lots of things well, but she's best at being a friend. Isn't it a senseless, backwards way of evolution? Don't we need to stop all that now, in the service of slowing carbon emissions and population growth? What purpose does loving as easy as all that serve, and don't you just hate the people who can do it?

So I turn my back, wordlessly, words won't help. I start walking, start running, the world blurs past me, a smoothie of Getty stock images. Faster and faster, and farther away, as — good news! the end credits of the film roll past. Goodbye, Evangeline — goodbye.

LIZ YEW

I am

Huewwwww. Huewwww. Huewww. I move as though it is my last day on
earth. I am searching. My mother rumbles her momentary wisdom as she
gathers her thoughts and swirls them around. She tries to convince me to
stay. But I am distracted. Hueww. My father beckons from far below.
Dry warm hands seeking my welcome. His soft breeze whispers in stillness
"come and we'll be together". I am searching. Huew. For my sister,
my blazing sister. Went and never came back.

LIZ YEW

This lady at the coffee shop

has a coffee to go every day

two sugars no ice she would say

eyes bright but never lingering

nimble fingers fidget with her ring

golden band worn with stories untold

never claiming attention but always bold

she nods with years of wisdom behind

every smile honey dripping from her refined

words as she whispers her thanks and strolls

away and goes onward as her life unfolds

one day there was not a chime at eight

in the morning with her worn band and

crooked grin and the world felt strange

it felt askew until someone else came in

golden band hung around his neck with

tender care and said I'll have what she had

KLARA SHER

New Gen 3: Sis

Content Warning: Gore

She walked across a corrie of barren rock; grey as asphalt that crunched
beneath her steps, not that she could hear it through the layered suit.
The Hedron cluster had always been an anomaly, a series of barren rocks in
space, yet they were contained in an atmosphere of violent storms. She had
longed to see them, touch them, she was the first to ever make it, a biologist
on a solo mission to catalogue the potential microbes here. It was habitable,
yet the severe weather and lacking resources kept people away, but not her.
She plodded along, in a blissful silence, her breath slow and deep as she
absorbed the landscape.

A storm was coming, or so the siren in her helmet decreed. How annoying.
She undid her helmet, feeling the satisfying suction and visceral click as the
helmet unrooted itself from her scalp. Silence. The air was too thin for noise.
She undid her spacesuit, feeling its tendrils unwrap from her appendages like
a reluctant mother letting go of a child; slow and drawn out. She was naked.
The air wasn't cold, nor hot. Her dark skin gaining a violet glow from the
atmosphere. It would be here soon. She breathed. The air was static and
stale, like a locked room which was waiting to be unlocked. She forgot
herself, her mission. There would be nothing here, even her body struggled
against the pressures of the air. Nothing would thrive. A shame, really, as
it was an isolated utopia in its storm clouds. She just stood and marvelled
at the violent arcs of lightning above, turning the dark flesh of the clouds
pink and serrating like a wound. She didn't know how long she'd been there.
She didn't care. She just walked and basked. Time wasn't a worry. After all,
when isolated in the middle of nowhere, on a barren rock which floats also
in the middle of nowhere, why would time matter?

But time wasn't the problem, it was the storm which had brewed since the rocks first formed. She looked up.

"Oh fuck!" she said, turning on her heels.

She sprinted, ignoring the stabbing shots fired by the rocky surface, the storm had almost snuck up on top of her. It's neon grin parting the heavens to show fractals of starlight. She continued to run. She could see her discarded spacesuit; this would protect her from the world she'd dreamed of. She approached, clumsily as the shifting gravity pulled her weight to different places. Her leg recoiled from a sharp stone, which caused it to collide into the other. Her body scraped across the Hedron's flesh, tearing her flesh apart in different ways, her blood watering the untouched land.

"No, no, no. Fuck. Come on! Come on, almost there!" She panted. Grazed and one foot out of commission she crawled, in infantile vulnerability, reaching for her suit, her safety. Her sanctuary. Her hand slipped across the visor, leaving a dirtied handprint of blood and rock dust on it as it was pushed away. She reached again. Her fingers tickling the glass. Then the world turned violet, then pink, then purple, then pain, then...nothing.

*

The creature opened It's eyes, head heavy and swimming with misplaced memories. It was curled into a ball at the basin of a crater. It was Its first day, yet it knew more than that of a new-born. It was as old as the world it now inhabited. What was It? It sat up and observed It's surroundings. The sky was overcast, illuminated with a vibrant tint of salt lamp hues, staining the clouds' flesh to an organic texture. The ground beneath their feet was dark, with a firmness beneath Its weight, yet had a few different sized other in a spiral. At the centre was a pink, raw tube, reminiscent of a tea towel being ringed out. It knew this but did not understand why, or what a tea towel was. The tube from the crater coiled across and into the stomach of the creature. It moved Its arms and stared, flexing the raw flesh of Its appendages, thin and veiny, over a carapace concealing its bones. Its membraned hands slid onto the tube and pulled at it, creating a squelch as the tube poured sludge onto the creature's stomach and then drained off into the crater.

The creature passed out.

The sky hadn't changed when It woke again. It looked past It's cartilage breasts and focused on the exposed architecture of Its organs, in a frame of curved bone and transparent flesh, a small crater existed where the tube had been pulled from. It looked around, the tube had withered and darkened, like dried seaweed. Why did It think of things in such foreign terms?
It pushed Itself-up, shaky, and uncertain. It knew what It needed to do, but Its body was still learning what the mind commanded. It collapsed.
It repeated the process for an unknown amount of time, passing out from exhaustion in between. Time didn't matter here, and so the creature didn't care. It tried again and again. Eventually It stood, uncertain upon the certainty of the world's flesh. It noticed two other tubes, withered, and curled on the crater's basin. It walked over and reached for one of the others. The surface turned to thorns and spiked Its hand, violet flashes stung Its mind and a voice screamed —

"They are not yours!"

It recoiled and collapsed into itself. I am the third sister. I am Three.
So, where are the others? She pushed herself up and began to grope at the crater as she ascended.

She stood upon the crater edge and breathed. Taking in the taste of the peach sweetness and oral dank of the static air. She could sense it; the planet was stirring, there was a storm brewing. She needed shelter.

CLARA EHLERS

Extracts from 'bearing fruit'

Content Warning: Sexual allusion, reproductive rights

the earth needs no more filling
she's full with men who tell me
I'm a "creator of life",
a right, "divinely offered",
"selfish", I hear them whisper on the street,
a "waste of potential gene-pool-parties",
"procreate, create a protean proletarian!"
I will not have my child commodified, comrade,
will not add my labour
to over-filled rooms
not my own,
but theirs.

mothers ripe with pride for their offspring, / not yet eaten

I could not bear to see my own devoured,
let me protect you, my precocious peach,
purely hypothetical hope of my mother,
let *me* swallow you whole,
like a Titan.
no teeth shall pierce our tender flesh
for we are one —
do not take root,

but let me ground you,
my changeling child;
exchanged, perhaps, with foolish pride
for love beyond placental bond
I love you, my unfinished foetus,
let not my love be tainted with unseemly seed —
remain only mine, a perfect peach.

mother nature's eyes, / winking, cheekily, caught in her trick.

for our mother is a sleeper agent
awoken by petulant patria,
infiltrated by propagation propaganda —
mother-tongue tasted father-land's false promises of liberation
enamoured with his flagging pride
whilst father bit her fruit,
raging war on her once luscious hills
be strong, mother, divorce paternal pressure
and lavish in the joy of impermanence — blossoming.

(This tree's value won't depend / on fruit it will not bear.)

MAYA ELPHICK

I Took The Pain and Christened It

To live with
a tight rib of pain
is mostly ceremony.
A ritual passed from mother to daughter,
to nurture and coax
the groaning weight
from the floodplains of your chest,
from the basin of your navel,
and naming it
a hot spring, a cupped bird.

I will make something of wings.
Release my body to the earth
and show me that every fruit was grown
so I do not starve
and every ocean exists just for me
not to drown in.
This world has given me so few gifts
that were not cut from my body to begin with.
I have had practice of
how to properly handle a mangled shape,
to self-soothe heartache
and balm a raw throat.

The sacrifice grows greater with each year,
to find holdings of warmth in fresh water
before it cools again and

to love vehemently enough
that life can not renounce you
this time.

MAX TODD

On melancholy hill

Content Warning: Suicidal ideation

I've always been fond of melancholy hill, despite being quite the ordinary place. It's actually a beautiful hill, but still ordinary, most beautiful things you see are actually quite ordinary. I suppose it's appreciating them that can be so rare, but that's not anyone's fault in these times. I can't stress that enough, you know, that it's not your fault.

The hill rises at the back of this park, just outside the city overlooking the urban megaliths. It reaches no extravagant heights, it's only a hill, but you'll surprise yourself with how out of breath you are by the time you reach the top. But I promise you will be rewarded with the most extraordinary panoramic view. You can see the whole city and wider suburban area, and if you turn on your feet even the great fields and wilder pockets of life learning to coexist with their immense neighbours are visible.

It's really quite ordinary, I'm sure you've climbed something similar if you really think about it, but this one, this particular hill was mine. My melancholy hill. Often I'd just sit there on this dedicated bench, watching all the people far away work through the windows, or the ones closer, playing football in the park. Depending on what time I get there, if I close my eyes I can either hear the birds waking up, the bustle of transport, or the voices of families together below me. It's a wonderfully melancholic hill, and that particular morning was especially so. I've lived this sort of life you see, it's got all the features of living, rather ordinary, not always so comforting. So I planned out this special day.

I wouldn't go to bed, I'd just stay up all night eating and dancing and lighting candles I'd received for Christmas three years ago that I was saving

for a special day. The ordinary is
                        quite sublime, if you make the right deal of it.
Sometimes you just can't, and that's okay too, but I'd really give it a go.
And then, just before sunrise, on a cool spring morning, I'd sneak my way
through the quiet city from my flat, and make my way up to melancholy hill
to watch the sun break open the night, rising in the east, illuminating my city
to the west. It's really quite ordinary, but it can also bring you to tears, it's just
that beautiful. A glorious sun waking the world you live in. And finally, when
I was truly satisfied, when I had recklessly indulged in all that I could so that
I could not fit any more love into my heart, I'd kill myself on melancholy hill.

Everything's okay, but I'm not that okay. I'm just tired. I'm not really tired
though. I'm exhausted. I'm just. So. Fucking. Tired. I just wanted to have
one great day before I go you know? The ink hadn't ran out of this girl just
yet, but to be honest, I just didn't see where the story was going anymore,
I really just hadn't the heart to finish it.

And that's okay isn't it? That's okay. It was not all bad, I had a good time,
I had some great times, I had some great friends, and I even had some
great family. But that's where I wanted to leave it, the hope I had for myself
had been fading for a while, so I made this plan. This plan to live with the
intensity of knowing I wouldn't see another day, see the absolute joy in what
I still had around me, ending it on my favourite hill watching a sunrise that
I'd never have to see set. And I was okay with that, it was a happy way to go
for me, isn't that what anyone could ask for?

So you can't imagine my disbelief, after working my way all the way up that
hill on my special day, that someone else, some poor boy on the grass, his
back slumped against the
                        bench, with those beautiful brown eyes cast open on
the city before him, had the same thought as I. He had walked the same
path as I, just moments before. He must've not bared to see the sun rise
again, he might not have had the strength.

I'll tell you one thing, I was happy to die on that hill, but when I saw his
face, frozen in his last happy moments, I think I found a new way to love.
Something about how he laid there was so peaceful, but made me so angry.
He was, of course, happier than he had been in life, but I would have given

anything to bring him back. He was real, ordinary looking, an ordinary boy, a beautifully ordinary boy. Love is in fact a feeling so alone you decide to die, only to find someone else has done it already, and you wonder to yourself why? Because I would've loved you. If I'd known before, I would've loved you too. Not with any inflamed passion, but with a resolute understanding of the tasks set in your mind. When I had fully taken him in, all of his happy, melancholic solitude, I sat next to him there. And like two kids discovering the meaning of a crush, I actually held his hand. I held his cold hand, and decided that the best thing I could do for him now was watch the sunrise with him.

RACHEL ELLIS

The Benefit of Foresight

Content Warning: Violence

Being with her is warm;
The heat a headstrong mountaineer feels
Seconds away from death, freezing in the snow.
The electric spark of her touch leaves
Frostbite on my skin.

Her hands are small in mine,
How one gleaming bullet too is also small,
And no marksman could fire a single shot
From his own deadly hands
And hope for better aim.

To touch her soft skin
Is to run my fingers along the leaves
Of spring-fresh velvet green, of stinging nettles and ivy.
I can let them choke my garden
Or rip them up for pain.

Her bright eyes gleam
Like oceans, like jewels, like flowers,
Like poison creatures warning through their flesh:
"I will hurt you. Do not touch, do not eat,
You brought this on yourself."

OLI HURLEY

"This Is You"

Content Warning: Medical Trauma

Before even knowing,
I was flying.
Before the needles,
Before the fingers
Placed on the page,
At my face.

"This is you"

Before I was you
I was me.

I could see
For miles, not
Think of the trails
Pushed into me.

"This is you"

A Prison
Where I bash
Myself on the
Wall. The
Finger pointing

Saying, this is
True. Lock me
Down, I cannot
Melt, cannot
Flow through bars like I
Used to.

Before the finger,
The cramped
Space.

Before the eyes
Locked onto my
Mind.

Vibrating in place

Now, constructing
The weights from
Their smiles.
In their Smiles.
On their Teeth.
Engraved,

"This is you"

MICHAEL BAKER

Cats, Reclaimed

The dinosaurs reigned for one-hundred-and-sixty-five million years.
But that's a bit of a cop-out figure, truth be told. In reality, that befittingly
monstrous amount of time was divided between five eras and untold
numbers of species, most barely related at all. And they only really got big
for the last ninety million anyway… Having said that, one must admit that
their lineage of carnage *did* stretch out further than humanity's entire history
laid end-to-end a hundred thousand times. So that's something. Their
predatory heritage is one completely unrivalled. Evolution has never since,
and may never again, enjoy such rampant and unabashed scope to run wild,
to experiment, to blow the roof off the planet with the howling gale of its
carnal orchestra. The dinosaurs were cool. Those that followed?
Rather embarrassing in comparison.

That is, with one exception.

Humanity made a name for themselves with fire. It was a clever little trick,
to be fair. Generate enough friction to turn wood into a gas then let all that
energy just sort of *whoosh* into a heated plasma. Free light, free heat.
Good deal. Who would've guessed where that little nugget of wisdom was
going to lead? A tapestry of brutality that would have made the dinosaurs
blush. All without weighing fifty tonnes or even a four-digit psi bite force.
Not to say that it was cheap. Over and over, innocent men and women
were turned into unwilling kindling piled on the blaze of progress. Again
and again, men and women were made betrayers and betrayed, their lives
written out in tragedies that would drag their descendants to tears hundreds
of years later.

"Yin must have Yang." "There can be no good without evil." "You can't have your cake and eat it too." And please, feel free to imagine and add any other platitude that the humans told themselves. They were pretty phrases, one supposes. But they all told the same blatant untruth with an innocent expectation of belief. Because humanity were not the exception:

Of course you can have your cake and eat it. The trick is just not being human.

Approximately eight thousand years ago, humanity began its slow crawl towards agricultural society. Everybody quite liked the idea of a regular food source that you didn't have to go hunting for. Seriously, *everybody*. The concentration of crops and harvest made human settlements a veritable paradise… for rats. The little blighters couldn't believe that the big hairless monkeys would be dumb enough to hoard that much food together in such a small space. The rats thought they were very clever as they swarmed towards the hunts. The irony of this collective opinion was not lost on the banditry guilds of cats that followed them. And they had a much better plan in mind.

Hunting crops from humans was a simple but often lethal endeavour. Hunting rats *for* humans was something altogether quite different. The thrill of the chase, the sweet, savoury-wet of blood on a barbed tongue. And at the end of it all? A saucer of milk and a scritch behind the ear. The rats thought they had found themselves a promised land. The cats knew better. They had found a business opportunity.

They made themselves pets. *Pets!* As if that invisible yoke pressed any meaningful weight on their lythe, powerful shoulders. But if ostensible submission was all it took to be fawned over, kept fed and given castles all their own to roam, then the cats would gladly play their part. As if they didn't choose it for themselves.

If the humans had been as discerning when it came to which other creatures they invited into their society, then their fate might've been quite different. Pigs, cows, sheep. Filthy things, really. It wasn't quite the same, of course; they weren't eating the cats. But then, if one had consumption in mind, all the more reason to (pardon the pun) better vet one's companions.

Inviting another animal into your home is one thing, but if you're inviting it into your belly, then you'd better make sure that they haven't picked up any sorts of nasty diseases.

That could be *quite* calamitous.

It didn't bother the cats when the hospitals overflowed. They weren't the ones that needed masks and gloves and goggles. Sure, the sirens yowling all through the night were annoying. But they were quiet soon enough.
It was of no consequence to them that the lights started to flicker, fizz, and die. They were silently glad for the chance to regain the strength of their flashing eyes — happy as their bodies once again felt the electricity of a hunt in a new concrete jungle.

It took time, bravery, and chance for the beasts of the wilds to realise what had happened. With tentative steps, the boars, deer, foxes, and squirrels alike began to adjust to the new world left behind for them. It was a slow process. They had to learn. To adapt. To wait as the natural order reorganised itself around the ruins. The cats had to wait for nothing. Their paw pads were silent on their accustomed routes across the fences and over the rooftops. Their fangs remind themselves of lessons learned in the rending of flesh and fur.

There's not much left of brick or mortar now. The trees have usurped the roads, and fresh dirt leaves thickening dustings of soil on the old paths of man. Unruly branches and vines spin around old power lines — the new highways of the cats that prowl the husks.

Just as the age of dinosaurs drew to its close oh so long ago, now too the age of fire has long since passed. The new age of the cats stretches out to lie in the sun, claws flexed and sharp. In the end, they didn't lift a paw to inherit the world.

LILY HYLAND

Everyman

Content Warning: Gore

He said 'noman'
and Cyclops knew.
They seek to conquer his majesty
by their blinkered view.

Wet with brains,
the sailors sat.
Blind to a peer,
they appear trapped
by the manacles of temptation.

Asclepian aims of lofty heights
were their poisoned chalice.

Two-eyed subjectivity:
Doubly complacent.
Parameters of possibilities placed aside, adjacent,
in Simonides' palace

Because,
simplicity is compelling.

Chunks of human flesh left
The Colossus
in a war of wit.

Of an army who came
to bury Polyphemus,
not to praise him.

Of flesh and fear,
meat and marrow,
limb from limb,
eye from socket.

E L L E N   N E W A L L

What I Gathered From the Stars

My choice to gather came to me every morning via the dawn outside
my window;
It burned so orange that it almost outshone the silver glow of my orchard.
I swam out to my orchard, holding my basket like paper;
I looked down (or up, it doesn't make a difference) and saw Earth
beneath/above me.
I nodded at the blue peeking from the eyelid-like clouds and returned
to my gathering;
I wafted in and out of the Gods and Goddesses, Kings and Queens that
made up my orchard.
From them, I gathered silence and peace of mind, gently peeling them off
in silver clumps;
I stopped at Orion and looked back to Earth, knowing that soon I shall
trudge, not glide.

MICAH PETYT

Strands of your hair

You know what's funny? The fact that even though you've been gone for
weeks now, I still find your hair everywhere. On my pillow, on the couch,
in the shower. And that's not to say I haven't been cleaning, because I have.
Once I could finally stand to let the smell of your perfume dissipate,
I scrubbed and vacuumed and laundered every inch of my tiny apartment.
It became obsessive, really. Like I needed to erase every trace that you'd
ever been here. And yet, here you are, popping up left and right,
like you never left.

About three weeks after you emptied out your things, I finally picked up the
book my ex had given me, hoping it might help me move on. It was the book
I'd been reading when we first met, remember that? The one with the pretty
blue cover. I don't think I'd touched it since you started sleeping at my place
more than you slept at your own. There, tucked between pages 152 and 153,
was a strand of pale purple. I'd completely forgotten that phase of yours.
That color feels like a lifetime ago, now. Back when everything was fresh and
exciting and new and nerve wracking. Back when I'd wake up to you still in
my bed, flipping through books I never bothered reading but kept around for
decoration, and I'd pretend to still be asleep because I was too shy to admit
that I couldn't cook for shit and that the best breakfast I could make you was
a bowl of oatmeal. Back when it felt like we had all the time in the world.

A few days later, I took out some towels from the linen closet, and picked out
a single blue curl. I don't think the blue lasted very long. Only about a week
or two. I loved it, but I remember you staring at yourself in the bathroom
mirror, wrapped in a towel and talking about how it washed you out.
We'd only labeled ourselves a month before, yet I already knew I was in love

with you. I don't think I ever told you that. It seemed too early to be deemed socially acceptable. When you showered, you always left the bathroom smelling of your lychee body spray, and I have to come clean, when I told you to leave the door open to let the steam out, it was really just so that the smell could waft into the room, and I could feel you with me after you went home.

Next came the red, in the folds of my sweater. The sweater I was wearing when I suggested you move in, while lounging on the couch after spending all evening sipping on wine and listening to ABBA on vinyl. If I could only save a single memory of our time together, it would be that one. Your head on my lap, my fingers twirling in your freshly cut hair, the plate of spring rolls on the coffee table and *Inside Out* playing on the TV, which never failed to make you cry. It was a random Tuesday night, and random Tuesday nights are what I miss the most, more than the museum dates or the walks through Lincoln Park or the kisses at the top of the Centennial Wheel.

You went back to purple a little after you moved in. A darker purple, this time. For some reason, I found that colour in Sappho's cat bed. It was the colour you had for the month and a half when you decided to get really into old periodicals. I found your collection in a box under the bed a few days ago. I know you forgot all about them. You left without giving them a second thought. I'd forgotten how shitty they all were. I'd also forgotten how often I told you that they were shitty. I don't know why your need to own mid-80's *Mad Magazines*, which you never read because you hated the humor, and so many *Sports Illustrated swimsuit editions* bugged me so much. After all, your eccentricities are what made me love you in the first place. Still, somehow, I can't help but feel like these magazines were the beginning of the end, and if I could go back, I'd buy you a couple hundred more.

You know what else is funny? The fact that I can write this whole letter filled with things I'd say to your face if I ever got the chance, while sitting in my car after finding a green strand on the passenger's seat headrest, and never actually giving it to you. My car is filled with your stupid magazines which I, oddly enough, don't want to get rid of anymore, and boxes of records you bought me and books you'd get more use out of than I would and clothes that I don't remember buying, which means they must be yours. My friends suggested that I burn it all. They said it would be therapeutic.

But I don't want therapeutic. I want random Tuesday nights and lychee body spray and hair dye stains all over the bathroom and dog-eared books on the kitchen counter and the soundtrack to *Dirty Dancing* blaring from my record player and stacks of magazines you never even flipped through and the clipping of shears and arguments over the best Pixar movie. Which is why I'm sitting here, parked on a random street in Wilmette, 20 miles away from home but less than a block away from your parents' house, writing this and wondering what the hell I should do next.

ROBIN J DANVERS

Ideal

First, start with a beautiful garden.
Then put two people, in love, who you have never met, right there in the
middle of the picture.
Try not to think about the house.
Try not to think about where you come from.

There is something missing from the things you want — you struggle writing
shopping lists and although you tried for years to have better handwriting,
you have never written an actual love letter. You have written apology notes,
birthday cards, postcards. No love letters.

And yes, of course, you had dreams about meeting someone. Who would,
inevitably, sweep you off your feet at a dance, suave, when your shoes match
the rhythm to the floor. You can dance, but can you name your emotions?
Are you the hero of this story or the love interest? Are you interesting?

You made another thousand stories featuring banter, outlandish characters,
zany quips, unusual happenings — ghosts, love affairs, classes, dinners.
Skip the parts where you're cooking, walking, sitting in your room-make
this story about one thing and make it fast.

Do you want somebody in your kitchen? I mean, really? Do you want
a husband? A wife? A partner? A co-pilot? Well, sometimes. Desire is a
funny thing. I think you must have missed the memo for it. I think maybe
everything is a little exaggerated in technicolour, or else you might be
colour-blind.

You want to feel better about yourself, and apparently if you know what people say about you and it's perfect, that does help. If everybody wants your brain and your body, that helps, but who do you want to be used to your shower habits? Relationships are like trips to space. Most of the time people come back from them, but sometimes they remember the stars.
In the same breath, it is also like moving away from home. I invented this person again for you to love. Reboot your childhood self and see if anyone wants to fuck you now that you're eighteen.

Your body is a wishbone, says God, and if you're lucky you'll meet a man who wants to snap you in two.

Of course, you want that. Of course you don't.
For once, you want to want something on your own terms.

RORY ELLIOTT-BRADY

Familiar

I know that I've been here before,
I've seen it all.
I know the times
Where you seem like you don't know me
Any time you catch my eye,
A place like this won't last that long,
I see it now, I know the signs,
You just smile though it's crumbling,
Still a king in your own mind.
I know these roads you've trapped me in
And I know that you do too,
They're shaped like the park that raised me,
They smell like apple juice.
You wrote a route on the maps we drew
And chained me to who I once knew,
All the stories that we wrote together
I now know to be untrue.

It's familiar here,
I hear laughs or maybe cries
Echo in these empty streets
Like children running by.
My feet have brought me back here

And I still don't understand how
It's smaller than I remember,
I can touch the rooftops now.
My world was thirteen square streets
Surrounding my old school,
The bus stop could bring me down the road,
At the end of the road was you.
I remember I felt so safe here,
I can feel you with each step I take,
I used to think I'd left long ago
But I come back, month by day.

I remember chasing after you because I could never run as fast,
I remember dreaming up those cities, and dreaming they would last,
For years I thought I'd grown past your hold on me
But any time I see a ghost of you, I become a ghost of me,
I used to think I could follow you anywhere
In your footsteps, always behind.
Now I don't think I could pretend to be familiar if I tried.

Only Music Moves Here

One of These Mornings by Moby played through one of my earphones.
Sitting down on the train back to Norwich, I tried not to think of the long
week of uni work ahead of me. I had spent the day trying to concentrate on
my essay before its deadline whilst balancing along the ever-shifting knife's
edge of serenity that exists in my family home. The train and I both let out
a sigh as it pulled away from central Cambridge. Familiar buildings and
bridges passed by. I thought back to my teenage years between them, the
long quiet evenings spent cruising around on my bike and the biting march
air along the banks of the river. Plugging my other earphone into my ear,
I relaxed and let Moby take me away.

The irregular clatter of the tracks and pitchy drone of the engine mixed
with the bold piano chords. Their steady pace held my attention as I began
to sway between the passing landscape and the music. I closed my eyes,
accepting the voice that rang over me, its vibrato calling me. The swaying
dissipated and drums fell in as the interface between my mind and body
shifted, their trajectory now destined along separate lines. As always,
I was there again, no longer rattled by irregularity, but surrounded by sonic
purpose. Within this new familiarity, the moving image returned to me.
It played over in a loop as the song penetrated my mind. But time didn't
matter here. The concept of repetition soon ceased to have meaning as
reality flattened, the moving image aligning with my consciousness. It seeped
deeper until the driving bass and I became one. My senses dissolved as the
barrier between sounds and sight blurred. The rhythmic piano took on
physical forms and the landscape materialised behind my eyelids. Before
I realised, all I knew was this moment as it spread to the edges of my reality.

Striped lane markers fell towards the car as they were swept beneath it.
Tall highway lamps pass in my peripheral like a metronome. Their cadence
is perfect, pulling me ever further inwards to the moment. I feel the mass of
my mind like a machine, its internal mechanisms breathing with it.
The road stretches out in front of the vehicle, gently curving into infinity,
a deep night sky peering back from it, swallowing anything that remains
outside of the music.

I'll never reach the end of the highway, but why would I want to?
It seems that my father will always be switching lanes, not that it means
anything, the road is empty. It's nothing but endless grey tarmac bathed in
sleepy tungsten light; a static moment in time, suspended within me, always
going forward. Only the lit road and highway barriers exist outside these
doors, the road held together in vacuum. My eyes stay fixed on it as it passes
swiftly under the bonnet.

I'm at the back of the car in the middle seat and my siblings must be fast
asleep beside me. But I don't look, I never will. The scene stays static in
motion and so do I. Light from the lamps wash over me like waves lapping
at the edge of my consciousness. It pulses over the car's interior illuminating
the leather seats. Their surface is painted with yellow vibrance for short
moments, disappearing and reappearing again in perfect time. Somehow it
feels separate from the lamps, as if the light's presence is a force of its own.
An entity communicating through brilliant colour.

Every pulse seems to beckon for my attention, revealing layers of
indistinguishable meaning and purpose. From somewhere outside, a deeper
texture resonates through my cosmos and the world shifts to the forefront
of my reality. I am now seated here, experiencing its phenomena as they
appear in front of me. Forms fabricate and disintegrate in the light, contours
of the seats shifting and dancing in my vision. They present themselves to
me in a newfound clarity, their language communicating a mirror image of
myself. Projections of coloured emotions pull me into a world of nostalgia.
Childhood ignorance, bewilderment and belonging expand from infinite
directions and I do too as the scene pulls me back into the past.

I remember now, I've been here before. The essence of my younger self
trickles through the pores in my skin, returning from a distant hibernation;

a part of me that is hidden under so many layers of ego that it's almost forgotten. Delicate notes of innocence ring through the light, its colours bolder than before. A new sense of value courses beneath them, singing with naivety. My spirit lifts out of its weighted slumber, floating with ease, naked in the unfiltered rays cast around me.

The leather seats to my left and right, the ever-curving tarmac beyond them and the steady beams carving their way through the landscape all move, exist and remain static. Only music moves here, it's the only thing that truly changes. I see it moving inside the very fabric of the world and feel it dancing outside the daydream.

Out there where it's less subtle, its shape dips in and out of recognition as I am suspended between the worlds. Layers cloud its dance in the real world, ugly figures cling to its sides, revealing the truths of a difficult world. But here, pillowed by early nostalgia, raw ideas expand from its textures. Simple lines and gradients communicate to me in their vulnerable vibrance, twisting in and out between the shadows and highlights on the car's interior.

I know that I can't stay forever, but I like to pretend. I long for my mind to align with the music, to exist here in its ethereal construction. Here, I can be blissfully ignorant to the bitter and changing geometries of a human life. I know that it can't be, that every time I enter, the end waits to beckon me back. I know also that my time here can only be grasped onto as a precious occasion and that travelling here through the music loses its value the more I do so.

The track ended, its volume gently receding as I was drawn back to the clatter of the rails and hum of the train engine. I fell neatly back into the hard texture of reality, its light hanging dull above me. I stared out into the trees that lined the horizon, my reflection, a lighter shadow amongst them. I focused my sight there and looked back at it. Eyes remaining still and lifeless, his complexion lost in the rushing trees. As the next track began and the train left the trees behind, his shape disappeared into the grey fields and I knew he didn't belong here.

LILY GLENN

Moon Jellyfish

dissolving, the dream
disappears into the
darkness of
my subconscious

half asleep,
my grip on Morpheus'
soft hand loosens,
razing fingertips

as I lean forward —
suspended like
an astronaut,
snatching

with the clumsy reach
of a sleepwalker treading deep water
towards the coiling tendrils
of a jellyfish

that glows with indifferent
effervescence,
carried away
by the currents of my mind

the dream slips away but
here it is again,
singing a siren's song
as it glimmers

yet my corporeal hands
don't belong here,
touching shattered
shards of silver glass

that reflect nothing but
the Aries moon,
full and high and
all knowing,

burning lungs smoulder
memory as I surface from the slow motion destruction
of a collapsing star.

NICOLE HUANG

Brain Gibberish

I am whole I am whole I am whole
Or am I?
Tis the damn season but I'm not ready
I hate to be wrong but also love the little flirty corrections
My brain is operating on gibberish and I don't need fixing
but at the same time I do

Come along with me shall we
I'm lonely and alone yet I'm left with infinite yearning, longing
I love myself and hate myself all at the same time

I'm always talking about myself
That's proof of the loneliness part by the way
I'll try to be better I promise
But self-indulgence feels familiar and I don't want to turn away from it

Fiction is too hard to write when I can't get out of my own head
my own world
If I can clone myself so I can do all the projects learn the vastly different
areas I'm interested in I would
I want to hibernate and rest yet I'm always restless
Is that even possible to be obsessed with other people's lives
while living your own
It haunts me to think how much love I'm willing to give

If I never see you again
Good morning, good afternoon and good night

KEIRA SIBBONS

Piranha Pond

Content Warning: Gore and death

Ever since I was young, I dreamt about finding a pond filled with piranhas. They were always coloured bright orange like the kind in children's cartoons, with sharp, white teeth dirtied by clumps of soggy flesh still attached. They swam in constricting circles, predators stalking their imaginary prey. Their scales shimmered even while under the ever-present overcast clouds that loomed above. Only the paper-thin dorsal fin along their backs ever poked out of the water, slicing the surface like signs of doom. They were small, as I peered down at them, the outline of the rest of their bodies was slightly blurry from being submerged underwater. Orange masses danced around in the otherwise pitch-black pond.

The pond itself was tucked down at the very bottom of a five-metre-deep pit. The walls of the pit were made of stone the colour of dry concrete, chipped and grooved like the side of a mountain. On the way down, ledges had been eroded into the stone; tufts of grass burst from them, like murky green highlights. I always pictured myself jumping down onto one to be closer to the water, but even in my dreams I was never brave enough.

The surrounding land was flat, stretching on for miles with the pit below as the only imperfection. It was the same grass that carpeted the ledges, just a darker shade, as if all the sun's light had been sucked from it. Through the mists that obscured the unknown horizons, there were silhouettes of surrounding mountains caging us all in. The sky above was constantly stuck on the verge of dropping into late evening, dousing the landscape in a hazy sheen.

I would sit on the edge of the pit and dangle my legs over. I never sensed that I was being spied upon, or that the piranhas below were glancing up and anticipating my plunge. Oddly, I was in exactly the right place there, welcomed like teeth to a piece of meat. I started to worry that the little guys were hungry down there. It didn't look like the pond fed into any larger body of water, so where could they possibly be getting all their nutrients from?

Suddenly, my arms were encircling a crimson bucket, which was filled with chunks of raw, pink flesh. Scooping a handful of cubes up, I held them at my eye-level, watching as a wet, red droplet crawled down my arm. It fell slowly, leaving a cold trail in its wake. Once I'd grown lethargic watching it, I threw their food directly down to them.

Waves turned as the piranhas all flipped over and lunged towards their meal. *Poor things must be starving.* Digging my hand back into the bucket, I prepared their next fill. I went on until the meat was all gone and there was no possibility that any fish could be hungry. Putting the bucket aside, I returned to watching them contentedly swim around in circles again.

Every so often I would have that dream. Somewhere in the back of my mind, I knew that if a whole body was to be thrown into that pond, the piranhas would surge towards it and rip all the flesh from its bones in less than a minute. After all, they were bloodthirsty and satisfied by nothing but their feeder and the other members of their shoal. Even as I grew up and learned that in a lot of cases, groups of piranhas wouldn't attack a body they sensed was much larger than them, the piranhas of my dreams remained in my head. Even as people in my neighbourhood started to go missing when I was a child, the piranhas were my responsibility to provide nourishment for in the dream.

Naïvely, it wasn't until I was much older that I started making the connections. The panic festered until I screamed into my pillow so much my throat was dry and torn from grief. But I knew it wasn't like anyone would ever believe me. I flipped between pacing back and forth in my room and throwing up and laying in my bed for days; but I knew that I would be forever burdened with knowing when someone around me was about to disappear.

At the beginning, it was people I didn't even know. And ever so cold-heartedly, it never affected me significantly. But then it was a kid I went to school with; the man that ran the shop on the corner; the lady who used to look after me when my mum couldn't as a child. Whenever I was faced with a new bucket in my dreams, I'd find myself waking up in a sweat the next morning. I'd walk half-alive through the next day, exhausted and red-eyed. I wondered if anyone made any correlations, if anyone in my life ever expected I knew something.

I was in a dream again, walking towards the pit where I sat down with my legs over the edge as usual. I peeked down at the piranhas' scaly bodies strutting through the water, waiting eagerly and expectantly. When no bucket appeared in my arms, I looked down into the pit again. Unlike any time before, there was a body standing on one of the grassy ledges. My own body, wearing the pyjamas I'd gone to sleep in. My face was passive and staring right back at me. Eyes neither sharp nor absent, mouth in neither a smile nor a frown.

Frozen, I watched as the other me turned away and faced the water, shuffling my bare feet to the edge. Because I knew what that meant. For the first time, I was awake in one of these dreams with utter clarity. The other me reared up, knees bent, expression calm, gazed at the depths of the pond with all its inhabitants one last time. I jumped.

Frogsong

Content Warning: Death

You're smashed grey, black against black gravel;
you lie there, limbs splayed. Still we see eye to eye.
Time has sucked out the corporeal juice;
rain rewets the wrong way. And so you died
unnoticed — unwanted even if seen.
A moment's thought to pick my foot over.
Like all, I don't want to touch the obscene
and what is more vulgar than exposure?
That is your death. Unknown what came before.
Like, what brought you to this grave paving stone
from the presumed green pond of nevermore?
Did you spend your watery days alone?
Does the air, darkening with time and smoke,
still hold the last note of your flattened croak?

EDEN GRAY

How to sail a bed

Content Warning: Depression and drowning

I never learned how to sail a bed   or why   to stay   afloat.
Black and blue   I   blue and white   never   ends
further   than any eye can be   seen,   splashing   crescendoes
against   the wooden frame thrashing, wind roars
                                            louder than blood:
      choking, near retching   gag   but   no   thing dislodges
                                                  no thing changes.
    Only   the scent shifts,   strengthens, putrid   and
pungent of pitiless   antiseptic would the   salt
suppress   the death-smell?   the world tastes
      the same inside and out,   hide,   clouds upon clouds.
          ice impersonating comfort,   lets make a pillow fort
will collapse   then I am to be   smothered.
Light laterdarkens: there are bruises   juice-staining   my neck everso   gasp
grasp   there is no thing left   sheets spasmed to shreds−
blue   blue   blue
                              blue

                                                        blue

Born of Blood

As the last embers of her campfire quietly crackled in the early hours of the morning and the first rays of sunlight began driving away the darkness, Isabella sat wide awake. Sleep had not found her yet. Instead, her mind spiralled as thoughts raced down into the dark abyss that was consuming her.

'They turned their backs on me… their own daughter — Where did it all go wrong?'

This same thought gnawed at Isabella, becoming a mantra thumping against her skull like a hammer to a nail. Each question she asked found no satisfying or reassuring answer. Instead, as Isabella finally stirred, she buried her head in her hands and sobbed.

She was raised in the Remulian Empire, learning of the Celestials who acted as guardians over humanity in life and death. From the priests of her village, she had learned to have faith in the Celestials but to fear the fallen ones seeking to corrupt mankind.

She was born under a dark star, an omen of being favoured by darker magic. In most nations, this meant little for such people but the Empire believed it was the sign of a great destroyer. Three days ago, Isabella's magic began manifesting, forcing her to flee her village or risk a brutal death.

Slowly stumbling to her feet, Isabella wiped away the lingering tears that stained her cheeks. Though she knew which direction to head, she knew little of the nations which lay beyond her homeland other than knowing that other nations were more friendly towards someone like herself.

Picking up her satchel, Isabella rummaged through the only belongings she had – a few coins, a journal, food and water for three days and an amulet that her sister had given her before she left to explore the world. Staring at the amulet, Isabella found herself lost in thought once more.

'I can't possibly survive on my own… I don't know how to hunt. I'll need to find a village and-and say I am a refugee or that my village was attacked by bandits? No… No that wouldn't work, they would ask for details and investigate… Keep it simple Izzy…"

Chewing her lower lip and furrowing her brow, the brief thought of finding the nearest Sanctuary of the Celestials crossed her mind. To throw herself before a Priest and beg their help. Yet, that thought quickly was shaken away, she knew the dangerous zeal that many Priests wielded.

With a deflated sigh, Isabella began walking, heading north-east towards what she hoped would be the border with the Principality of Brigadon. Yet, as her boots squelched through the mud and dew-covered grass, Isabella's thoughts were halted by a piercing scream nearby.

Freezing in place, Isabella looked around, wild-eyed as if expecting someone was coming after her. A few seconds passed with pure silence, long enough for Isabella to begin wondering whether she imagined the scream, before it pierced through the quiet morning once more. This time, Isabella was focused on her surroundings, noticing the addition of several men shouting and screaming in a language that she couldn't quite make out.

While deep down she was terrified, Isabella's curiosity got the better of her, weaving through the dense foliage of the forest before finding herself at the edge of a grove with strange standing stones dotting its perimeter, carved with mysterious runes.

Yet, her attention quickly turned towards the sight of six armed men surrounding a Half-Elven woman, an Elven man and two young Half-Elven children. Though she couldn't make out the conversation from here, she could tell the Half-Elven woman was trying to beg the men before being bashed on the head, crumpling on the ground with a cry.

As one of the men raised a mace towards one of the children, Isabella found herself rushing out closer towards the men. "Stop it! They're unarmed and helpless!" she screams, fighting the urge to flee in terror.

"Stay outta this, girl! These creatures are getting the justice they deserve, they do not walk in the Light of the Celestials like we do," said one of the men, yet all six turned towards Isabella, seemingly startled by her sudden arrival.

At the mention of the Celestials, something inside of her snapped. Whether it was from the strange power emanating from the standing stones or simply something manifesting within her, Isabella screamed — the sound booming powerfully across the grove.

Gasping for air, it felt as if all the oxygen in her body had been sucked out of her. Her body felt numb, leaving her falling to her knees. She was not sure what happened at first, nor why the men had not attacked yet — until she saw blood marring the ground around her. Looking up, each of the men lay on the ground, blood drained from their bodies with some even missing their heads. It was as if all their blood simply escaped from them.

Letting out a gasp, Isabella stared in horror before looking towards the unharmed family before her. "I —... I didn't — " she stammers, shaking her head in fear.

"It's okay, you saved us. You didn't do anything wrong," said the Elven man, his voice filled with an almost fatherly warmth. It was a tone Isabella did not expect to hear ever again from someone. Stepping closer carefully, the Elven man slowly embraces Isabella while the girl remains stunned by what was happening.

"Your magic may be a curse here, but your Priests are wrong about it. There is a beauty to all magic — no matter what form it takes on, even Blood Magic like yours."

Slowly, Isabella found herself calming down. The fear and adrenaline slowly faded from her body as exhaustion overtook her. As she felt herself slowly slipping into unconsciousness, Isabella felt something she had not felt in days, maybe even all her life — acceptance.

"You're safe now girl. Rest, we will bring you with us…" the Half-Elven woman whispered softly as Isabella fell asleep.

NAOMI SABEL

You should be wary

Content Warning: Abuse

You should be wary
of little girls who watch
with sullen eyes in corners of rooms
who don't speak much
because you wouldn't like
the things they'd say.

They grow up to smile in polite company
and seethe silently behind closed doors,
in the shadows,
choking black on hatred for
the things you've done.

The rage of a quiet woman should be feared above all:
it lingers when you think she forgets, it keeps watch, it is
insurmountable.

You men, you think you have all the power,
but it is the women
exiled to doorways for hours,
smirking into their wine glasses
filled to the brim with derision
who could unposition you.

You are cruel to things you don't understand
which is why you are cruel to me.
You cannot complain;
you gave me your fury.

And I don't want
to talk to you;
I don't owe you anything.
Blood is not bondage, it is a coincidence,
a catastrophe.
What did I do to deserve you?
What did any of us do to deserve our fathers?

I could cry for you,
but what would it do?
I have wasted enough tears on broken things
without wasting them on you.

M.J.J.MACDONALD

How to Wash Socks

Content Warning: Gore and animal death

I dropped my tights and looked afraid
Your car was by my laundromat
"Eat apples till they break your teeth
And throw up in my fancy hat"

I packed a bag for Sacramento
Sprinkled sugar on my fate
Then I dressed up like a lady
On a high stakes hostage tape

You chased me onto buses
And I punched you through the flies
Did you dissolve above the belt?
Was that my Kubrick eyes?

You lost my scent in Sacramento
While you whistled through the crowd
I kept on turning left
I want to die inside this town

You killed my dog, I cried in shapes,
He smelled like thoughts and tears and bleach
I was barefoot and infertile
By the time you let me sleep

I smashed a vase in your left finger
Bled infection into maps
We took presents for the doctor,
Why's he screaming in his hands?

And with the sourness of vomit
    Spreading thickly in my cheeks
        I realised the bugs in my peripheral
            Had not been real
                or weeks

I nudge myself polite
They have names Plato can't conceive
And if they break into my house
I'll say that I'm asleep.

WILLIAM MCKINNEL

The Wooden Chair

Content Warning: Climate anxiety

It stared at me: a faceless gargantuan product of times long gone; no signs
of life at all, except for the pain. The pain that it feels every day due to the
torment that it is forced to endure. It has lost everything... its dignity,
its wisdom...and now its life. It has died before its time, and the burning
hatred that it feels cannot let it find peace — until it has its revenge.

I ran my hand along the arms, feeling the cool smoothness of the wood,
trying not to hear the agonising screams of slaughtered trees vowing
revenge; trying not to picture the demonic smile of Man as his saw ripped
into their souls. As his hammer and nails twisted their once majestic bulk
into a sickening parody of a wooden Frankenstein's monster.

His varnish silences their screams, only for them to be replaced with a desire
for vengeance. The chair shall be a gift, says he, for a child who is ignorant
of the ways of the world, or for a fat-bottomed lord. How much shall we sell
it for? One pound? Five pounds? One hundred pounds?
All the wisdom, all the divine knowledge, all of the hope, all of the good in
both Man and Nature gone... for a handful of coins.
The chair does not dare disobey, but it remembers.

One day, Man's shackles that keep nature in check will break,
and all that will be left is the eternal hatred of a former slave.

WILLIAM MCKINNEL

Time Heals All Wounds

Content Warning: Extremism and murder

The man who destroyed humanity.
Here he was, right in front of me.
I had the chance to kill him before he could do it — but one question
burned through my mind.
"Do I have the right?"

My name is unimportant, but what you should know is that I have travelled
back in time fifty years to save you all. Not that I expect any gratitude,
but you deserve to know how close you are to being erased from existence.
His name is Theodore Finch, and he was, and is, one of the greatest
scientists humanity has ever produced. You might call him a genius,
if genocide is acceptable to you. His only crime was that he was a genius,
and he felt that he had to prove it.

One day, a seemingly ordinary day, war broke out between the nations of
Earth, and no place, no people, were safe. We were broken, desperate,
and exhausted people - poverty, sickness, death, and loss had taken us to the
brink of collapse. And like the Good Samaritan that he was,
Theodore Finch scratched his colossal brain.

He infected us. With a virus. Not your primitive flu virus, but a virus which
would kill the average human in a matter of hours. He called it an
"act of mercy," believing that in war, no one was innocent. He believed that
the "impure" needed to be eradicated so that only perfection could
rebuild humanity.

It was not a particularly pleasant way to die; at first, you felt a small tickle
at the back of your throat. Ten minutes later, you coughed up blood.
Twenty minutes later, you felt a blow hit your chest with the force of a
sledgehammer, your insides boiling with the ferocity of molten lava.
After that, death would certainly come, but when… I do not know.

My wife did not know, as she lay on the ground, choking on her own blood,
desperately gasping for air, neither of us knowing that we would lose
each other forever.

As I stare into his coldly analytical but oddly childlike and quizzical eyes,
I tell myself that I am doing this for her. For you. But I wonder if I am.
After ten years without love, with only a handful of mutated, abandoned
souls for company, the hatred that I feel today has lived with me for so
long that I can't remember feeling any other way.

I was rescued by someone who travelled through space and time,
and who was the first person in what felt like an eternity to show me
kindness. Whether he was human or not did not matter; his society was built
on tolerance, a singular respect for all life, and hatred was a thing of the
past. Feelings that I had thought to be long gone resurfaced; the first true
happiness that I had felt in a long time. He showed me the kind of future
that humanity could have had… that I could have had, if hatred had not
blinded me. But I was determined to never feel loneliness again. He was my
mentor and friend, and I betrayed him.

I had to abandon the man who was kind to me so that I could find
Theodore Finch to stop you all from becoming like me.

I stood behind him, watching him work feverishly with the eccentricity
scientists seem to be born with. He was every inch the absent-minded
professor, with the shock of frizzy hair, the glasses perched precariously
on the end of his nose, and the jolly smile of a grandad.

He took a sip at a cup of hot chocolate, one of his "sneaky vices",
he said to me with the smile of a child at a sweet shop on a Friday afternoon,
humming a song that sounds vaguely familiar to me… Bryan Adams'
Living on a Prayer.

Upon meeting me, he shook my hand with such warmth, with a joy buzzer
to match, that for a moment, I forgot that I intended to kill him. But as
I look at him now, consulting the Periodic Table and illegibly scrawled notes,
humming a song belonging to a time that is closed to me forever, I see his
smile and his laughter frozen in time, seemingly mocking me, and I feel
something so painful that it's making me lose control. It's as if the laughter
will never stop, and logic demands that I destroy the source of all my pain.

But do I have the right?

There it is again. The question that makes me human again. If I were
to kill him, I would be no better than he is. What would she think of me,
murdering in her name? I realise that my hatred stems from shame,
the shame of what I became, and what I did whilst claiming to be saving
humanity as justification for my actions. I'm hoping to dump all of it on
Theodore Finch, hoping that the pain will go away. So that I can live
with myself.

I took a deep breath and made my decision.

I do not think that he was an evil man; I even forgive him, and myself,
for not realising this until too late. To quote Friedrich Nietzsche, he was
"Human, all too human."

ELEANOR DAVIES

"Get It Done"

Band   aid
       Fate on the tongue
            S t r e t c h i n g   as a   landscape.

You will never do it well enough.
You haven't yet, just look at it.

          So,
            plunge or rip or grit and moan
            shred the whole thing screaming for your mother
            push against and pull away, yank and yank and
            unleash and blitz and cry as it crumbles.

       Get.   It.   Done.

          Is what I did.

Only for the chess pieces and walks around Eaton Park to stick to my body
and burn at my scalp. For my work to be derailed at the 'Chinese Takeaway'
sign. I was buying milk. I cried, stood still on the pavement and everyone
was fine but me.

EJ WALKER

A Standard Interaction At Work

The scent of the confectionery store reaches them first. Their past few minutes escape them: a journey towards an integral volta; a journey interrupted by a pit-stop, just to pick up a brownie or two before they continue on their designated pathway, or catch their designated train. The scent clears their mind. The future can wait. The place to which this shift in direction would lead if they could just keep moving —

A bell rings as they force the door open, and step inside, and stand.

Can wait. Stationary, before they are tugged in by the sweet sharpness that had halted them. Awash with purple hues carrying the palette of salty effort playing with the clasps of their coats and the rain dripping from their hair, the shop stacks itself with mounds and hills of produce. It's difficult to discern where one colour begins and another merges with it, and mingles with others, and clumps, and spills.

Archibald prefers them like that, but he tends to forget that many customers don't. Ah well. That memory won't stand the test of time, nor, he predicts, the scrutiny of whoever hears their tales.

Accompanied by complaints from his chair, Archibald emerges. An older gentleman, with a freshly-pressed shirt and whose colourless hair juxtaposes the vibrancy of the room. Before Archibald reaches the customer, catching them by the shoulder, and leading them to the counter, the customer might just catch a glimpse of the confectioneries dividing themselves. The windows don't show the rain that still drips from them and wets the floor, nor does it audibly pelt the roof.

'Ignore that — alright! Name's Archibald Gale.'

Archibald remembers the hands he shakes, calloused and creased with
the memories and the time and the rot. Always wet with rain and, thus,
obscured. Time has a habit of doing that. Time demonises him.
'Now, what can I do you for?' Because he offers a service. He offers his past.
He offers a respite from the swift tides invoked by that beckoning, ideal place
that the customer always needs to get to, and soon. Before they can squeeze
their hand from out of his, he proclaims 'why don't you come and scope the
store out, my friend.' They oblige.

Any replies are usually about the state of the store. These statements fizzle
out once they catch sight of the neat rows of dishes and bowls and cases,
the produce now behaving itself. Curlicues decorate every wall and surface,
hiding the cracks forever travelling along the splattered shades of the wall.
The cracks were there when Archibald got the place. He likes to think
he owns it.

The customer lurches forward and into the bulk and grasp of the store.
Archibald perches atop the counter, pats shoulders and watches them go like
a parent would to a child starting school. The customer opens cases, inspects
the flapjacks working together to maintain their neatly-stacked positions.
They prod and peck at the merchandise lining the walls, checking for other
glitches in the matrix of their vision. They never find any.

If Archibald had it his own way (and, of course, if the customers received
it well), he'd rather like some sort of iconography or logic-defying stunt
to show for angering the very fabric of Time itself. The customer will
often find themselves lingering at a certain item, a certain scent, a certain
sheen. Some ask. Some don't bother. He approaches them anyway, often
disappointed that they didn't break the long-standing record for the shortest
time taken to stop pacing.

'This here was, in fact, my own creation,' he says, every time. Every treat was,
in fact, his own creation. 'This one took quite a while to perfect, so its many
versions have been on my store-front for a long time. Has that longevity,
you see. Lasts through changes in taste and changes in demographic.
You know what mean.' He doesn't quite know how long this product has

been there. He doesn't know which pieces converse. They may be his
creations, but they move forwards. He doesn't. He superimposes in the drawl
and diatribe assigned to the piece they have picked out. They stare.
They continue pacing.

They pick up. They put down. He flinches in response, not for his own pride,
but for the subject of their scrutiny. They don't notice the squirms and
screams products emit as they're picked. The positions of those stacked in
piles or on display at all are determined by brashness and bravery —
or, rather, stupidity. This is integral to his punishment, he supposes.

They stop once, twice, thrice, peering at the display cases. He is well
acquainted with the process of waiting for them to decide. Or not.
Waiting without the feeling of time whistling in his ear as it passes.
He watches others collecting their goods, moving towards that one place to
which they are pulled, or dragged, or forced. He is chained by the thing that
frees them. He had only wished to skip forward a little, to discern his own
future. Time doesn't seem to like that. And now that future is just out of
reach. He can only weld the stasis. Pitiful, isn't it?

Products materialise within the customers palms. They walk over and place
the wares on the counter, ready to be charged and surprised when they
aren't. Archibald has no use for currency, although it would be interesting to
collect and compare. Anything to mark the time that doesn't pass.

As they return to the rain that doesn't fall here, the bell sees them out.
He has learned to tune its toll out. 'You enjoy that, you hear!' Archibald
shouts after them. They sometimes reply rather ironically, but they're always
in a hurry. They spent way too much time within the store, but it'll become
apparent soon enough that their designated transportation or destination
has waited for them. He wonders what that's like.

He resolves himself to waiting for the next customer to step inside and stand.

BADRIYA ABDULLAH

Thoughts of a Possible Insomniac at 3am

You should talk to someone.

~~You should fall asleep before this music stops playing.~~

You should watch your lecture in the morning.

~~You should transfer your notes to paper.~~

~~You should undo, wash and dry your hair in the morning.~~

You should. You should. You should.

You should call this piece, "Thoughts of a Possible Insomniac at 3am."

You should make this a list poem.

You should do this more often; it's making you feel better.

You should check the date later.

You should call your family.

~~You should hold yourself accountable for calling your family.~~

You should start spilling out your guts at night.

You should tell him you love him more often. (Father).

You should tell her you love her more often. (Sister).

~~You should remember a passing thought.~~

~~You should stop when you run out of 'you shoulds'.~~

You should reread this moment of time, right now.

You should love your mind more, since you value it so much.

You should visually organise your week to help yourself cope.

~~You should have stopped when you felt satisfied.~~

You should be grateful that you gave yourself time to think.

You should push through for a few more days.

You should tell yourself, 'I love you.' more often.

You should cross off the things on this list that are unrealistic.

ZOE MOLLOY

Considerations We Reject

April

I consider myself increasingly nervous as we roll around
Back and forth, 12 after 12 to April again.
It holds weight, meaning that no theorist can understand. April is
The month that my words grew faces, where dreams festered in the
tight mixing pot.
We met Vincent, sitting alone, he thought of how he could become better,
as we watched him thinking he was god.
And Margot looked at her decorated arms, wanting to ruin her creator's
reputation. Her god's inner self-reflection.
Our desire to survive glowed too brightly. That we stole, and fought,
and breathed in each other's faces out of spite. The segment when music
eliminated fear, ignited sentences, ignited brighter existential crises.
I knew that this was my month of evolvement,
just hoping
everyone else could see it.
Yet no one will know, the weight we hold, sitting as the sun sets earlier,
in the time we begrudgingly call April.

December

You think this is when it all comes to a close
A final era to reward or reproduce yourself for your next season. No.
December read us danger, we climbed down, huddled in a cave.
A capitalist scheme built levels below ground.
Running and whirring, injecting, and manipulating as long as their
accounts keep rising.
Out of reach
We grasp!
December means no end for these actions, no resolutions will be sought
after The Ts and Cs are too small to read, as the new year brings the
same consumer habits
As we eat with flourish, consume with greed
We become dependent on this new rotation
Yet we are tied to our dependency on the injected flesh. You are not the
man, you are
Consuming
Underneath him
The snow falls softly over head, as we sing and wrap, unwrap and consider
How these will take place in our everyday lives
Until she realises that those she thought were her twin pillars, turned her in
To the man

July

We sit, the two of us. The grass creeps into our system,
growing out of our pores
I see a kind creature who sits, hazily, across from me.
Beautiful Visage.
The middle, summer, the heat rolling over our organs as we melt.
I wish to melt into him, know how his blood runs differently
Still since he arrived, it has shocked me. Still trembling
To my core. And still now as I tell myself
Riddled with guilt,
That I am letting him die.
He will soon become a man, who held more beauty, and fragility
Than I had ever seen in any woman before. His heart frightened me,
urging me to be kind
The way he can.
Yet if I can be kind, then he can be cruel. Although,
Never in this lifetime. Where we sit
In the grass, half naked in the sun. One with the earth, so deeply connected
To its roots, that we are no longer two individuals.

ZAMEEL JIBRAN

FUSE MY REMINISCENCE

Past is an untold fiction
Where the whole of wax scattered
Around our reminiscence.
It is a broken penitent,
Para of our passage,
Which is more ambiguous
To the bibliomaniac
Who is curious for palpable candour.
I wish to voyage to my past
Where I could fuse
My scattered past to consensus,
Without having any guilt
Of being a catastrophe creator.
Although it is unravelled and unheard
In our contemporary phantasm.

ZAMEEL JIBRAN

MANIFESTATION OF GOD

A glimpse of our past
Whisper of our future,
Or divination of existence.
Someone called her deity,
Although she composes
Herself as an allegory,
Without true elucidation.
Her endearment
Discrete our fiction,
Her ardour exemplifies
Divination of art,
She crumbles our intuition
Cherish our wisdom,
But she is a manifestation of god
Always riddle.

SEE ME

Content Warning: Sexual violence and harrasment

I am looked at.
Stared at.
Don't worry, my mate's just interested.
He wouldn't do anything.
He doesn't bite. He won't lick his lips and leer at you.
He won't try anything,
Not until you're drunk at least,
Not until you can't say no,
But come on, don't be so rude, he's a good guy deep down.

I am overlooked.
Looked past,
Looked over,
Looked up and down
Stared at,
Too scared
To say
Stop.
Well, I shouldn't have worn a skirt if I didn't want to be looked at.

I am looked through.
Seen but not heard
Everybody looks at the man
Who knows what he's talking about
And who are you, his wife?
Are you good looking?
Looks like you lucked out
Lucky you
But beauty isn't forever, remember, you'll have to swap her out

I WILL BE looked at but never learned.
I WILL NOT trust you or your words anymore.
I AM Smarter than I look.

RACHEL SIMM

Chalk Circle

I was blind to the chalk circle he had drawn around me.
He loved me until I made a mistake. Stepped out of the chalk circle,
Wore something he didn't like.
I was reprimanded. I must stay in the circle,
And I learned well enough how to stay put.
Until he drew the line closer and closer. Until just standing was wrong to him,
So I stood on one leg.
And then he got rid of the circle completely,
And told me to get back into line.

HATTY HARDY

Apple Tree Swing

Life grew in that golden garden;
The one with the apple tree swing.
Thick frost draped in December,
And daffodils danced in spring.
Lifeless leaves lay in September.
But the sweetest sight by far,
That swing on each soft summer night,
Soles sweeping against the stars.

HATTY HARDY

Nobody Noticed Her Fall Apart

Content Warning: Violence

Trudging through the sharp, stiff silence,
A quiet in the still; the vociferous violent
Voices oozing, from within, through her skin,
Pores tearing, tears pouring, eyes bleeding,
Blinding her with it. Snaking around
Bare feet, up, up. Binding and bone —
Crushing. Shattering the once stained-glass,
Crawling further, thick smog fills up her head,
With a burning chest and bleeding lungs.
Her body feels so small,
And everyone else at the party,
They don't see anything at all.

MAX WRIGLEY

London Freedom

I let them riot. They're flocking near the bridge with a mainline station
nearby. Manned by the British Transport Police, no doubt it'll end soon.
I don't want to get involved. Neither do I want to be a witness. I walk on
by, past the River Thames, to the other side of the embankment. It's a fresh
morning in a summery London. The temperature's still high, mid-heatwave.
It's better than a downpour or snow. Hell, anything's better than a downpour
and snow in a city. I enjoy spending my mornings by the London Eye before
I become bogged down by a busy day. Heatwave or no heatwave, when
I see blue sky and no clouds, there's one thing that I know for sure:
the sky is open.

BARNABY HILL

Bed

Content Warning: Sexual themes

My mind goes straight to the loving,
        your
            tongue
        butterfly-fluttering pearl,
dripping with your sumptuous words;
                    these sheets are too beautiful
            not to be ruined
to not crush the velvet the wrong way,
to leave ruched up scratch marks,
        dark,
                soft
        and
                vulnerable in
the wet hearts of love bites
        curating a jacquard print of small roses
of supple moans pressed into
indulgent pillows
and
        tasselled throws
knotted with curling fingers,
into fabric utterings of
        hot breath

and ruby-stung cheeks,
        peacocks and emeralds
crisp and   ever refracting
tenderly drawing in the tart touch of flesh,
        bursts of your serenities into this embroidered night,
        let me tease   apart those golden threads so
fall back into my small kingdom,
silken cushions, kissing you to a balm,
the plush palace of worship,
        a thrum tuning you from cerulean to dubonnet and opalescent,
in this room we can invoke a fabricated Heaven.

BARNABY HILL

Church

Content Warning: Sexual themes

You speak with the righteousness of someone who plays victimhood like a sport / And I thank your god I'm no longer bound by him / We're the bastardisation of his image / So fuck you fuck you fuck you / Fuck your holiness / Your piety to a rapist self-crucifying god / Desperate to immortalise himself / In cadavers in ejaculate alabaster in crumpled cans in feigned alcoholism in a personality patented by Stella Artois / What a pathetic idol you've thrown your life before / You won't be remembered as a disciple.

AYESHA AHMAD

From Darkness to Light

A nocturnal being,
I rise at night.
Lured by the dark,
I step out of the light.
The comfort derived from the darkness is undefeated by any other
Because that's when the tiredness of the day I finally smother.
Let me tell you the story of why night stopped frightening me
Instead, it ended up enlightening me

*

I often found myself out after sunset,
Wandering the streets, the thoughts trapped in my mind,
my subconscious slowly let
Out of my head.
Nature's beauty reminded me how insignificant I really was,
In this web of life
This reflection deepened the strife
Within myself, stirred up the turmoil.
Heaviness took over,
I gave in to the weight of my struggles,
Sat on the curb,
A loneliness began to disturb.
And then a stranger passed by and offered a concerned smile
It didn't go unreciprocated

That one smile I really appreciated,
It's the little things that make you elated
Just like that, I felt better
Walking the next mile.
Night-time doesn't always blind you and seek to prey
Remember the glare of the moonlight?
It manages to make a way.

FREYA CALCUTH

I.

I.

a buried verse

The human condition is so fragile
and inconsequential;
we will all be buried under
layers of earthly fleece
or have bones set alight in
coffined sanctity that our
mourning children pay for —
if we even achieve that much

II.

Neither dead or alive;
somewhere in between.
For now, a breathing corpse
like the soldiers that went to war.
A gentle reassurance of what will remain.
A graveyard manifests inside
with touches of death's silence.

III.

sweaters; dirtied and frayed.

our love grew out like
the sweaters we wore as children
(dirtied and frayed); a bit too tight
at the edges. and just like my
favourite sweater; i'm scared
of tired limbs outgrowing you

your fabric stretched until
the uncomfortable revelation
scratches at the heartbreak
of our slow, painful demise
(clothes hangers in dark closets)

i will look you in the eye,
my own crumbling with tears,
playing with the hem of hearts:
*(why can't you just love me
the way i beg you to?)*

IV.

lips stained red; a lioness
devouring doe-eyed prey

licked lips in sweet desire
little red tore the wolf
limb to limb to find grandma

ELIJAH WILKINSON

The pebble

Whilst walking on the beach,
I found the most remarkable pebble.
With each corner riddled with mystery,
and an exquisite hope beaming from its gloomy teeth,
mangled and entwined with a sort of,
demotivated redness.

It truly was a remarkable pebble.
A ponderous box, oscillating in my hand,
as if I held a magnetic wooden hut up
against a pure magnet,
and it spun like neon through a sign.
The luminescent guilt of some other world, yet still…
It sits in my hand. Untouched, unscathed.
A cacophonous shell of archaic thinking,
coated in a thick layer of mystery.

Or perhaps it is some sort of icy medallion.
A gift, no, a reward!
For the trial of the senses,
valid to the vulnerability,
sewing the distance between the streets below and the sky above,
frozen from an age built onto with concrete,

derelict and destroyed,
still holding every memory but blurred by the irritating sounds
of the modern day.

A daydream of illustrious terror,
flabbergasted by the ship-in-a-bottle society they have created.
The envelope of the sky is torn and
opens to reveal a dark grey desperation,
shrouding the periwinkle fields that lie below.

It could be tossed back into the sea,
to be forgotten.
They think nothing more of that
remarkable pebble,
At peace it can finally rest at last.
Forgotten by the future
and remembered by the past.

or maybe,
as I toss it back into the sands, it's just a
pebble.

MUSA JOHNSON

My air ballon is cold.

Content Warning: Depression

This is concerning,
As I was hoping
Not to be put In a cold air balloon,
But a hot air balloon.
This is because A cold air balloon
Will not rise.
I tried rubbing my hands together
To warm up my cold air balloon,
But I only grew tired.
And so did my air balloon.
My air balloon told me he was depressed,
Because he didn't feel hot enough,
And had performance issues.
So I sent my air balloon to a shrink.
The shrink however,
Only tried rubbing her hands together
To warm up my air balloon,
As words don't tend to radiate heat In the same convectional tendencies
On which hot air balloons rely.
This did not work,
She grew tired.
So did the air balloon.

93

My air balloon confided in me,
That he was jealous after seeing Led Zeppelin on my walls.
I reassured him that this was no real
Floatation device, and rather, some musicians
And a Plant, perhaps a daffodil, perhaps a succulent;
I am not sure.

RHODA AKINDELE

Unrequited? Yes, or no?

Why aren't we dating?
I feel the muscles in my cheek tire as you speak,
attempting to hide how you constantly make me smile.
If I was melanin deficient,
I'm sure my flushed cheeks would bait me out
I'm sceptical, I'm sure you know I want you
Delusional.
I convince myself
you're equally scared to make the first move.
So afraid and crazy in love
Exuding confidence, powerless at the thought of potential rejection.
But here I am...
Waiting for our love connection
I'm already connected, hiding under the guise of friendship.
I want it to mean more,
when you say, you want my heavy thighs.
Don't just hype me up
Tell me you love me
Lemme know that I am enough.
Confess you've got the same tight feeling in your chest
Here I am losing breath...

95

When you wear that one black sleeveless vest
Sorry, I really like your arms
I'm obsessed, let's hold hands
Continue to take me around, but let's make out
Let's alleviate the tension
Remove the questioning
Keep the romance.
For now, it's seemingly discreet
Let's be bold,
Mate, our next meet?

Life is water

Life is water. Life is a tidal wave. Life is an ocean.
It's vicious. Powerful. Has layers of secrets.
But once we learn to sail and swim, we can conquer it.
We no longer have to stay in shallow waters.
Wondering what we may see if only we dared to venture further.

Instead, we can sail for miles.
We no longer have to stay on top of the water.

No longer have waves battering us; no longer have floats restraining us;
no longer have people watching us.
Instead, we can take ourselves under.
We could go so far that the water is still. Calming. Beautiful.
We can mourn the loss of treasures swept away in the evening.
Or we can still write our names in the sand; still admire history behind the
broken shells — capture the moment; treasure the memory.
Because when we see beauty in the world, the world sees beauty in us.

The University of East Anglia's Creative Writing Society
~
Committee 2022/23

President: Barney Hill
Vice-President: Helena Keys
Secretary: Klara Sher
Social Secretary: Oli Hurley
Equality & Diversity Officer: Ellen Newall

With an extra special thanks to our editors:

Ayesha Ahmad
Clea Licht
Clara Ehlers
Claramae Jones
Elizabeth Yew
Freya Calcluth
Laurel Brown
Lily Glenn
Max Wrigley
Micah Petyt
Naoise Gale

Cover design by Gemma Pugh
Instagram - @gemmagia.illustration

Egg Box Publishing 2023

www.ingramcontent.com/pod-product-compliance
Lightning Source LLC
Chambersburg PA
CBHW051812050726

47598CB00006B/2532